PERSUASIVE
BUSINESS
PRESENTATIONS

To my parents

PERSUASIVE BUSINESS PRESENTATIONS

A practical handbook to help you sell your ideas to groups through the spoken word – more powerfully and profitably

Nick Robinson

MERCURY

First published in 1990
by the Mercury Books Division of
W.H. Allen & Co. Plc
Sekforde House, 175/9 St. John Street, London EC1V 4LL

Set in Baskerville by Phoenix Photosetting
Printed and bound in Great Britain

British Library Cataloguing in Publication Data
Robinson, Nick
  Persuasive business presentations: a practical handbook to help
  you sell your ideas to groups through the spoken word – more
  powerfully and profitably.
  1. Businessmen. Public speaking
  I. Title
  808.5′1

ISBN 1–85251–053–6

Contents

Introduction

Hello, my name is Nick Robinson . . . and welcome to *Persuasive Business Presentations*. First, I have a confession to make. You're reading this book under false pretences. Do you think it's all about how to speak persuasively in public? Well, that's part of it. But we're also going to do something together which is far more useful. And that is, to explore ways in which you can increase your company's profits, enhance your own career and develop your own potential. Now if you could at least start on that path by the time you've finished reading this book, would that be a good investment of your time? I hope so.

Bold ambitions! But it *is* possible to go far in achieving them, simply through developing your skills in business communication. A survey by *Fortune* magazine asked the Presidents of top US corporations what course of training had been most important to them in their career. The overwhelming majority (72 per cent) cited public speaking: the ability to communicate ideas, often to a hostile or sceptical group, and to gain their support.

Nothing in this book is untested theory. It's all based on my own experience of what works and doesn't work. I've led 240 seminars on advertising and PR in the last five years, and made every possible mistake in speaking to groups of ten to five hundred individuals. (I even invented a few impossible mistakes.) I'll reveal those errors so you can avoid them.

I've also led, or been actively involved in, over 300 sales presentations to smaller groups of two to ten people, during the last ten years. With some very skilled colleagues, I helped build a public relations consultancy from nowhere to a place among Britain's largest. It meant winning a lot of presentations! So I'm starting to have a feel for what works, and what flops. At least . . . usually. A fact you learn to accept when making presentations is that a few snafus are inevitable, and to be taken in your stride. (A snafu is a Seriously Not Appreciated Foul-Up.)

Let me give you a preview of this book. Relax, it's a short book – you can probably complete it in an evening or two. But to ensure you get maximum value for money the subject matter is very condensed. Why not make the book 'your own' by taking notes of key points as you go? At the end, you will have built your own Action Plan, a guidepost to brightening your company's future and accelerating your own career.

Hold on . . . what's happening here?

Did you spot a pattern in my text so far? First, I tried to *gain your attention* – I said you were reading this book under false pretences. Then, I *promised you a benefit* – successful speaking can enhance your future. Next, I offered two *'proof statements'* – a survey by *Fortune* magazine, plus a description of my own credentials. I gave you a little *preview* and *timetable*. Finally, I again *summarised the benefits* you should gain and pointed to the future.

Does that sound suspiciously like a pattern for the start of a good business presentation? It is. Let me come back to that pattern, and how you can use it successfully, in just a few pages' time. But in the meantime, you can see that a professional presentation has a structure, much like a good textbook, and you can quickly learn it.

Summary

Presentations need a structure! Try this one:

- Gain your audience's attention.
- Promise a benefit.
- Offer proof statements.
- Give a preview and timetable.
- Summarise the benefits and point to the future.

Eight ways to banish the fear of speaking

'Jeremy Bullmore must be the finest public speaker that the advertising industry has ever produced . . . And yet he suffers terribly from nerves. I have seen his hand shaking as he perused his notes . . . he felt that if he failed to feel nervous, then his speaking skills would have deserted him and he would have to pack it all in.'
Chris Wilkins, *Marketing* magazine

Nine out of ten people rate public speaking (logorrophobia) as the greatest fear in their lives, greater even than death. Do you? I certainly used to. Perhaps it's because we expect the audience to laugh at us, to belittle us with facetious remarks. And yet, in a business presentation at least, *this virtually never happens.* Even the worst of our presentations will be met with politeness. So why do we make such a fuss about public speaking?

Imagine you're in the pub with half a dozen colleagues and it's your turn to buy a round of drinks. So you take everyone's order, then distribute the drinks. Did your knees shake with terror as you addressed them? Were you afraid to speak in public? I doubt it.

Now, suppose a big contract is at stake. You have been

selected to present your company's case to the customer's board of directors. Some of the powerful people at that meeting are hostile to your company. Yet your firm's entire future relies upon your persuading them to your view. Now, are you afraid to speak in public?

I hope so. Unless you feel a little nervous in that boardroom, you probably won't give your best! And yet, the difference between the two occasions is all in the mind. We can all walk a plank that's laid on the ground. Lay it between two buildings 100 feet above ground, and the mind rebels. Every time we speak in a group, that's public speaking. Most times, it doesn't worry us. The problem is that even a group of two can terrify, when it becomes an 'audience'. *Audiences – not groups – are the problem.*

How does a group become an audience – and how can you use audiences to your advantage?

Mounting to the lectern triggers the body's fight or flight reaction. It's the best time to have a tooth out. It congeals the mind, dries the blood and numbs the body. (Quite literally so – it closes the capillaries and shuts down the pain receptors.) There is probably a good biological reason for it. Our genetic memory tells us we have reason to fear the unbridled passions of the mob. If the current of the room is hostile, all there will eventually be affected by peer-group pressure. Burn witch, burn!

But group-think can be good news too. It can be your best friend, if all goes well. It shifts the undecided, motivates the apathetic (*sieg heil!*) and gives you – metaphorically speaking – an honorary key to the club locker room. Where the choicest deals are made.

So welcome nerves. That extra adrenalin will kick-start

your brain and fine-tune your performance. But panic is not desirable. Here's how to banish panic by sound preparation before the event:

Rule 1: *know your audience* – a known quantity reduces the panic. (See p. 24.)

Rule 2: *dispense with the audience* – rehearse three times. Preparation is 90 per cent of the work, the rest is chemistry and luck. (See pp. 58–9 and 67–9.)

Rule 3: *assume that everything will go wrong*. Paradoxically, that is meant to be reassuring. Prepare for crises and prepare to weave crises into the show. Then, when all goes well, you might even feel a bit let down! (See pp. 72–5 and Chapter 7.)

Each of these ways to minimise your risk *before* the day is explored in more detail a little later. They do help to eliminate last-minute panics.

But what about controlling your nerves at the event itself? Let's imagine the Chairman has announced you, and all eyes are suddenly on you. You stand up and . . .

You are standing up, aren't you?

It doesn't pay to make presentations seated, even with just a few people at the boardroom table. You lack authority and control. A secretary bustles in with coffee and . . . you've lost your audience. (Of course, you may want to emphasise your non-threatening attitude, such as in a free-flowing creative session or a union bargaining situation. Then it would pay you to sit down, and on the same side as the group.)

You take a deep breath and fill your lungs

(Not too deep or you'll hyperventilate and fall over.) Having full lungs is important because otherwise your nervous tension will stiffen your diaphragm – giving you that 'butterflies in the stomach' feeling and a voice like Donald Duck's.

You relax into a stable body posture

Have you ever watched a martial arts film? Then you'll know the judoka 'ready' position, both feet evenly balanced, legs eighteen inches apart, one leg slightly before the other. It's perfect for presentations. With it you can make gestures, twist and move your body without fear of stumbling. Even aim a jumping side-kick at the tea lady . . .

But don't rock from side to side like an elephant digesting a meal! (New shoes are bad news. At presentations, they tend to pinch because your feet swell.)

You've probably seen speakers who take up defensive

postures. We all do it at times. Particularly to be avoided
are the:

Duke of Edinburgh (hands behind back): It makes you
look (and feel) like you're facing a firing squad.

Napoleon (hand tucked in jacket). What are you
scratching in there?

Archbishop (hands clasped in prayer over groin). It looks
shifty.

Urchin (hands in pockets). You're tempted to jiggle
change and your studied casualness insults your
audience.

A continuous straightening of the tie and checking one's
zip are signs of a nervous male speaker. (Check zips and
buttons first, then forget them!) Ladies tend to put their
hand over their breast or constantly fiddle with jewellery.

Ask a colleague or spouse to tip you off to your nervous
tics. Ideally, film yourself on video. You can rent a video
camera for very little nowadays. It's a sound investment,
because all such tics distract the audience from its serious
task of voting you money.

A lectern can help to hide these distractions, and conceal your trembling fingers, nervous hand-washing and
fluttering kneecaps. But the lectern is risky in business
meetings. It's too reminiscent of the pulpit, the lecturer
. . . *you want people to feel close to you.*

If you're presenting to a small group, abandon a lectern. You'll be amazed, too, at the impact you'll make in a
large conference if you have the confidence to come down

from the platform and – mobile microphone in hand – continue your address while walking among the audience!

Another confidence-building tip is to pack a personal emergency kit in your pocket: comb, aspirins, Rennies. And if you'll be joining them individually later, Amplex. Next to opera singing, nothing poisons your breath faster than public speaking.

You start by thanking your introducer, then you pause

Smile and look around. Let the silence stretch a little. (Three seconds will feel like three hours.) Silence quietens the whispers. Let them decide they like you before you open your mouth. First impressions are visual, not auditory.

During this long silence, psyche yourself up

Tell yourself, 'the audience is on my side'. Actually, it probably is. Even if they're glowering at you, they want to feel their time won't be entirely wasted. Good driving instructors tell novices who are nervous of traffic, 'Don't worry, they don't want to hit you any more than you want to hit them.' This may not work at political rallies, but it applies to business speaking.

You also deliberately recall previous occasions when your presentation was a triumph. You know your material is good. You do have such memories, don't you? If not, acquire some at once! Seize non-threatening opportunities to speak, at staff meetings or social groups. Soon you may even come to enjoy speaking. (For some veterans, the adrenalin buzz they get after making a good presentation is its own reward. Winning the business is a bonus . . . At this stage, of course, such folk should be hastily pensioned off.)

Most important, you'll build up a bank of peak moments, positive memories of successful presentations you have made before. Invoking these memories – like practising your golf swing in your mind – will itself improve your skills.

Use the ideas above and you will find that you can control the fear of public speaking. You may learn to like it. *Lo, you may even become a logorrophile!*

Summary

- Research your audience in advance and script your presentation accordingly.

- Adequate rehearsal helps banish nerves.

- Assume that everything will go wrong and have 'fall back' options in each case.

- Stand up to command confidence – both yours and the audience's confidence in you.

- Take a deep breath and fill your lungs.

- Relax into a stable body posture.

- Start by thanking your introducer, then *pause*.

- Tell yourself the audience *want* your presentation to succeed. In fact, they do!

2

How to read the body language of an audience

'An audience is two people or more with the power to vote you money.'
Mark Twain

We were talking about the power that groups acquire when they become an Audience. We'll return to this topic in detail (see pp. 24–6), where we'll explore ways to script your presentation so it has the greatest appeal to all the different 'sub-groups' in your audience. But for the moment, let's assume you haven't had the opportunity to research your audience in depth before your presentation. Suddenly, you're on stage. What can you still tell about the audience, just in your first glance around? Are they hostile? sceptical? apathetic? Or are you lucky enough to find them friendly? supportive? enthusiastic?

You can tell a lot about how receptive your audience is from observing the way they sit at the outset. If they don't know you – and particularly if you're trying to sell them something – most will have closed body patterns.

A	HOSTILE	SCEPTICAL	APATHETIC
B	FRIENDLY	SUPPORTIVE	ENTHUSIASTIC

A well-structured presentation allows
the audience to move from A to B
without appearing to 'persuade'

Signs of an unresponsive audience

Arms crossed. Hand over mouth. Fingering lips. Eyes
closed. Studied inattention, including reading something
else. Frowns. Tense shoulders. Sly asides to their partner.
Leaning back in their chairs, eyes on ceiling.

Don't worry at this stage. Frowns reveal objections.
Excellent! Even hostility is to be welcomed. Why? *At least
someone's responding.* You have a good chance of handling
the objection and advancing the sale. Little is worse than
unresponsive silence. It does not necessarily mean your
cause is lost, but it can kill your morale.

Incidentally, beware that new phenomenon, professional buyers who have been on a body language course.
They use practised gestures to unsettle you, particularly
when you talk price! I remember one who frowned, slowly
shook his head, straightened his papers, pocketed his pen,
checked his watch with horror and said 'Your fee is out-
rageous. I don't know how you blighters have the nerve.'
Crestfallen, we were packing up to go, when he added
with a twinkle in his eye: 'When can you start?'

You can also learn a lot about an audience by noting their positions in the room, assuming they assemble simultaneously.

How seating position can reveal the management hierarchy

The most confident and dominant members will take their place in the front of the room, or at the end of the boardroom table. This usually includes the boss. The next in command take flank positions beside the boss.

Have you ever noticed that a family at the dining table sits in the same pattern? Mum is next to the kitchen door, Dad takes the dominant head of the table, and the oldest son sits beside Mum – staking a claim on her in a Freudian challenge to the father. So watch who flanks the boss! They need special attention too.

Side positions denote underlings. Bosses will rarely take corner positions at their own conference table, and will also expect to take key end-table positions at *your* conference table. By careful. You can make important people very uncomfortable by putting them into flank positions and/or assuming the boss position yourself. This is not helpful in a sales presentation. But it can be a useful tactic when negotiating with a supplier.

Usually, difficult people – hecklers, critics and cranks – take positions at the back or nearest the exit, as if saying 'I'm not really part of this occasion. And I can escape quickly if I have to.'

If you can control the room layout, this can subtly help you to handle a group in the way most appropriate to your purpose.

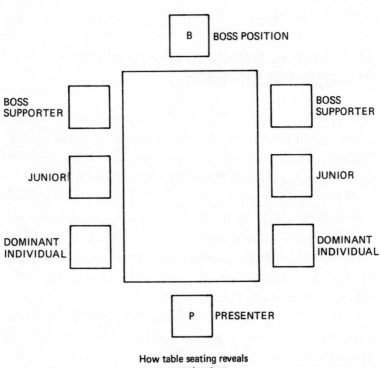

How table seating reveals
power structure

Controlling group response by controlling room layout

If you're talking to a large fractious group of dealers or shareholders and you don't want too many hecklers, go for theatre-style seating. It conditions people into a receptive mode and is also very uncomfortable so they won't want to protract the session.

But if you want maximum interaction, go for round tables. Little villages of four or five people take root, talk

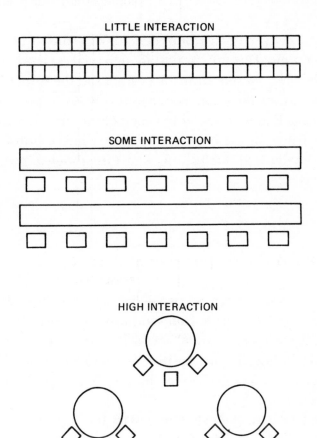

Room layout can control
audience behaviour

together, develop rivalries with other tables and gain the confidence to talk back to you. Sometimes endlessly.

Boardroom, U-shaped or classroom style are best for long presentations where notes must be taken. But beware: a boardroom table will sleep fifteen. And frequently does. All but the first two guests can hide from the speaker's eye.

Generally, largish groups do follow Parkinson's Law of Receptions. The most important figure takes centre stage, other VIPs assume strategic positions in the corners and the courtiers float aimlessly about. *But you cannot count on this Law.* Every presenter has the experience of the 'funny little fellow in the back row who kept interrupting' and was finally told to shut up, who turned out to own the company!

Signs of the responsive audience

It's not hard to tell when you've moved your audience from level A to level B, from a negative to a positive mood. You'll see them: leaning forward, arms open on table, head nodding, making positive noises to their neighbours, smiling . . . Even if they disagree with you, they're listening.

But beware the eager beavers who – smiling all the while – take reams of notes. It's a power ploy. They usually will click their ballpoint very noisily at the end. Then, attention gained, pick you up on some point of devastating inconsequence.

How to get an audience on your side

To move your audience out of apathy into enthusiasm does not necessarily mean being flamboyant in your delivery. I once watched an American sales trainer come badly unstuck when addressing a group of British estate agents. He started with a vibrant 'Hello' followed by the cheery appeal 'Aren't you all going to say hello to me?' The audience's embarrassment was palpable, and his presentation flopped. What works well in New York cuts no ice in the conservative boardrooms of Europe!

Instead, developing your audience's rapport with you may depend upon many, many small things. For example, people prefer to buy from people who are just like them (or are just like they'd like to be). So mimicry is important when making a business presentation. Here's how to use it:

Dress reassuringly

You're asking for money! 'Power' dressing is a serious business. The darker your suit, the greater your credibility. Men should check the styles currently being worn at the House of Commons or the Institute of Directors bar. (Window shopping at the local Round Table is not the same thing at all.)

The 'in' style for men now is white collar, striped shirt, dark blue or red tie with regimental stripes or small square dots, plus matching handkerchief. Do not wear a light grey tie, you'll be mistaken for a waiter. Bright red ties can also upset conservative customers.

Ladies will know better than I whether to soothe their audience with a sombre Maggie Thatcher suit or to slay them with haute couture.

Both sexes should beware of distracting jewellery. Remove chunky cufflinks, jangly earrings or bracelets and large belt buckles. They distract and clatter, whether or not you are 'on mike'. It makes you look like a shady property developer. Needless to say, keep your jacket on.

One exception to this Rule of Sobriety is when the Rule of Mimicry takes precedence. If you meet separately with the customer's technical or creative people, discard your jacket. Wear short sleeves. Display a rack of pens in your breast pocket. *Above all, carry a clipboard.* But do not do this when the board are present. It relegates you to technician level and someone may ask you to fix their computer.

Respect their territory

Can you remember times when a sales executive called on you and lit up a cigarette without permission or perched his feet on your coffee table or moved your furniture without asking or sat in the boss's chair (yours)? Probably you didn't say anything, but his presentation to you flopped.

We all have a strong sense of territory, and you can use this to your advantage. For example, making the presentation in *your* office removes *their* power base, and gives *you* psychological leverage. (Customers should prefer to come to you, anyway. How else will they confirm that you do not operate out of a back room?)

If you do operate out of a back room, a prestigious

rented venue can be worth the cost: like the Design Centre for a novel technical idea, or the Institute of Directors or House of Commons for just about anything. At worst, rent the boardroom at a luxury hotel. A neutral venue can give you more leverage than presenting your case at their premises, where they have territorial control.

Acknowledge and thank them

In a small group, you can acknowledge them all by name before starting. If you don't know them all, simply say 'Let me just check that I understand who everybody is.' And repeat their names and job functions, checking with each as you do so.

If you do know them, be sure to bring all of their names and titles into your introduction:

> 'As you know, we're here today at the invitation of John, your Managing Director, and in the last few days we've had the pleasure of talking with Bill in Marketing, Jane in Research, and Joe in Distribution . . .'

In a large group, acknowledge the common bond you all share:

> 'We all have a strong interest in convertible loan stocks, which is why I feel the next twenty minutes will be of particular value to us all.'

17

Promise a timetable and stick to it

> 'In the next 35 minutes, we will explore xxxx. That should allow some ten minutes for discussion and the formal presentation should be finished by 10.30 am.'

This is a courtesy. It shows professionalism. And it relieves those who hate meetings, and have full in-trays. Of course, if the question time strays over, that's up to them – you've kept your promise.

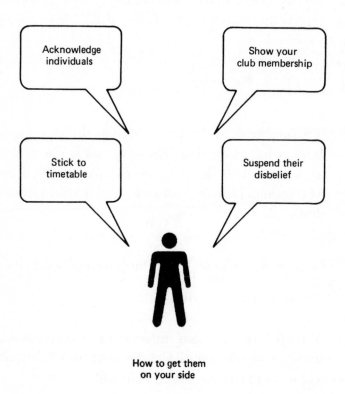

**How to get them
on your side**

Remind them of your club membership

You don't need to be a Freemason to show them that you're a member of their 'club'. You'll dress like them, of course. Talk like them. But don't forget to *tell* them that you're just like them. Refer to a mutual acquaintance, your membership of their trade association, your introduction or sponsorship by an accepted employee. It also helps to have a friend in the audience of whom you can ask rhetorical questions:

> 'You remember when, John . . .' or 'Isn't that true, Jane?'

But be sure of this person's standing in the group (a few discreet questions during your preliminary research should establish this). If you're seen as merely the puppet of an unpopular employee, it will alienate those who can't stand him or her!

Use an appropriate speaking style

Apparently, there are five types of person, in the sense of how we prefer to process information: Thinkers, Feelers, Viewers, Listeners and Readers. Reassure your audience at the outset that they will be able to Consider, Imagine, See, Hear and Read things during your presentation. You'll keep their attention better!

Of course, you'll also make sure to include elements of See, Hear and Read in your visual aids.

Suspend disbelief at the start

Promise you will give proof of everything you claim, by citing third-party evidence, or special research, or client testimonials:

> 'I will show you evidence of how Vauxhall Motors have cut their stocktaking time by 12 per cent, and saved some £400,000 each year.'

These are all proven ways to 'get the audience on your side', to move them from a negative to a positive mood and to reassure them that they'd like to do business with you. I'll come back to some of these points in a moment. They're so important that (like the key points in *your* speech) they deserve a little repetition . . .

If you make a business presentation, that usually means a big sale is in the offing. A big sale starts a relationship. And customers – all things being equal – prefer to buy from a supplier with whom they can relate well. As human beings.

How you say something can sometimes be more important than *what* you say! This is why I have started with how you should face an audience, i.e. how you should establish your credentials as a human being. In the next chapter, we'll look at what you actually say.

Summary

- Seating position can reveal the management hierarchy.
- You can control group response by controlling room layout.
- The responsive audience reveals itself through body language.
- To get an audience on your side:

    Dress reassuringly.

    Respect their territory.

    Acknowledge and thank them.

    Promise a timetable and stick to it.

    Remind them of your club membership.

    Use an appropriate speaking style.

    Suspend disbelief at the start by promising proof of what you're about to say.

3

What to do before you prepare your presentation

'To persuade an audience, find out what they believe in. Then tell them they're right.'

Franklin Roosevelt

If you want to sell round-the-world cruises to members of the Flat Earth Society, you don't talk about 'global' tours. You simply assure them they won't fall off the edge. If selling computers to administrators, you don't tell them their procedures will become obsolete at a stroke. You show them how their existing procedures will become more efficient.

Don't waste your time trying to change the belief systems of your audience! Christianity has had 2000 years to change the belief systems of the world, and it's still working on it. Instead, show how your proposition *reinforces* their belief systems. To do that, you have to know what their belief systems are. Probe your audience with these sorts of questions, as long as possible before your presentation takes place:

Compile an audience profile

What are their average age, seniority, reporting relationship, job function, experience level, attitudes to you, attitudes to your proposal? This will tell you how much they are likely to understand the benefits of your proposition . . . and what their objections will probably be.

It will also determine your sub-groups. In a meeting of three people, there are three sub-groups. A meeting of thirty is more homogeneous but still there will be five or six sub-groups. Often far more, rarely less.

For example: if you're selling a production system which is more costly than their existing system but 30 per cent more productive, you may be presenting to the Production Director, Commercial Director and Personnel Director. Any one can veto it. Each person clearly has different needs from your system, a different level of understanding of it and is likely to have different objections to it. Each person is, in short, a different subgroup.

And for success, each sub-group must be appealed to in a different way.

List your sub-groups

Note the biggest benefit your proposition offers each subgroup and what is each sub-group's biggest fear. (An objection is really a fear in disguise.) For example, when selling PR consultancy services, we typically present to:

Sub-group	Main perceived benefit	Likely objection
Marketing Director	Better awareness in market?	Best use of budget?
PR Manager	Reduce my workload?	Threaten my job?
Sales Manager	Increase sales leads?	Waste my people's time?

When your customer discusses the benefits to their company of your proposition, remember that they are also wondering: 'how will this enhance *my* job security or status or income?' Customers are human. So for each sub-group you are addressing, list as well the benefits which will accrue to the *individual*.

For example, these could include 'enhance my career prospects', 'increase my salary', 'give me prestige among my colleagues', 'secure my job if the contract goes through' . . . Of course, you wouldn't make these points during your presentation in such crass terms. But you would find oblique ways of putting these ideas in your audience's mind, perhaps by referring to individuals at other companies who – quite incidentally – benefited in this way.

Discover who else is presenting

My consultancy once gained a large new account, in competition with a far bigger consultancy, simply because we asked the client beforehand who else was presenting. Sometimes the company will tell you. You lose nothing by asking!

In this case, knowing our competitors, we were then able to predict the style of presentation that each would make, the strengths they would highlight and the weaknesses they would conceal. Then, in our presentation, we systematically showed that such 'strengths' were not apt to the client's needs and that they frequently hid weaknesses which could prove dangerous. Needless to say, we didn't name our competitors!

When you can truly act as a 'consultant' to your audience in this way, by seeming to help it make up its mind, you have a powerful edge over any of your competitors – provided, of course, they haven't done their own research beforehand on you!

Summary

- Compile an audience profile – so you are addressing a *known* group.

- List the sub-groups in your audience – each has different needs to which you must appeal.

- Discover which of your competitors are presenting – so you can predict the points they'll make and discreetly pitch your presentation to scupper them.

4

Painless ways to write your script – the Opener

A hired speaker was attempting to address the sales conference but was continually interrupted by cries of 'Rubbish' from one sales rep in the back row. Turning for help to the Chairman, the speaker was drily told 'By all means carry on. It's the first sign of intelligence that chap's ever shown'.

Every persuasive presentation must get a response – *it must change something* – or why do it? Even a staff briefing meeting is not merely an exchange of information. It should also raise morale and change staff attitudes, enabling them to become more committed or more efficient. Or why hold it? Of course, a sales presentation actively seeks an order or permission to proceed further towards the order. When writing your script, take these preliminary steps to sharpen your presentation:

Define what you want to change in the audience

What can people reasonably do as a result of your presentation?

For example, do you want them to recommend your company as a supplier to their colleagues? Or place the order then and there? Or shortlist you for a further presentation later?

What can you reasonably expect to change?

For example, you won't convince that Flat Earther we've met that the earth is round. But you could reasonably change his mind about taking a world cruise. That way, point out, he could check the facts for himself.

What can you achieve in the time available?

For example, you probably can't sell a million-pound machine in five minutes – you would need a multi-step sale involving many presentations. And you can't normally do much at 5.30 pm on Friday other than obtain commitment for a longer meeting later. But that's still an advance.

Have different objectives for different sub-groups

Your answers to these questions define the purpose of your presentation. But the purpose may vary according to your sub-groups. You may require them to do different things. For example, if presenting a **PR** consultancy service, you need to change the mind of your sub-groups like this:

Sub-group	You want them to
Marketing Director	Choose you (not others)
PR Manager	Confirm your professionalism
Sales Manager	Demand PR help (yours)

How to structure the script

Apparently, researchers have determined that the ideal length for a presentation by one speaker is seventeen minutes. Other researchers have suggested that leaders of industry have unusually short attention spans. They are capable of intensive bursts of concentration. But don't ask them to sit through a two-hour spiel!

Of course, a solo act by a gifted speaker has been known to keep a seminar audience enthusiastically awake all day

– with the help of frequent changes of pace, audio-visual diversions and a lot of audience interaction. But that is not a sales presentation.

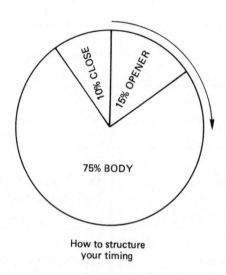

How to structure
your timing

If you go on much longer than seventeen minutes, you increasingly expose your audience to Randomity Deprivation Syndrome (boredom.) So let's assume the worst case, that we have only a few niggardly minutes. How should we structure them for maximum impact?

15 per cent Opener: captures attention and previews material (2 mins)

75 per cent Body: reinforces material with evidence (14 mins)

10 per cent Close: summarises, recommends and calls to action (1 min)

Your whole presentation should, in effect, be a call to action. So one minute at the end is enough to remind them of the specific steps they should take now. If you have several sub-groups in your audience, be careful to remind each member or sub-group of the steps *each* should now take.

For example, you might suggest that the Commercial Director confirm the savings promised by your product against the company's actual figures. The Production Director would be reminded that you will deliver product samples next week so he can test them himself. And the Managing Director might be advised that you will be calling him at the end of the month for his decision.

Let's take a closer look at the three elements of your presentation, the Opener, Body and Close.

The Opener

Paradoxically, this may not be the best place to start! At least, when writing your script. Many speakers find it useful to write the Opener *after* the Close. The Opener previews the whole but you can't preview anything until you know the ending. Besides, writing the beginning and end before the middle defines a sort of bookend structure to your script, disciplining its contents into a neat symmetry. So try writing the Close first, then the Opener and only finally, the Body.

Your Opener exists (a) to gain Attention, (b) to Preview your presentation (it sets the agenda and reassures the audience it will be relevant to them), and (c) to establish your Credibility (what are your credentials to address us? Why *your* company?)

The entire Opener is often best done by another member of your team, who can say flattering things about you which you couldn't say yourself (so establishing your Credibility). Changing the speaker after a few minutes also keeps interest alive. And it establishes a smooth structure: the Opening speaker can move in again after the Body of your presentation to Close and ask for questions.

How to gain attention

Do not fire a starting pistol. Speakers have actually done this and people do have heart attacks. Nor is it wise to stage an accident (although the time I tripped over an electric lead by mistake and blew a fuse worked so well that I tried to keep it in my presentation thereafter. To no avail.)

In my advertising and PR seminars I often start with very arresting music – which I then relate quickly to the matter in hand. ('Wouldn't it be nice if our advertising also had the impact of Beethoven's 6th?' 'That was *Carmina Burana* – a piece of music that's full of excitement and heresy. Just like today's seminar!')

This is rarely apt in a small sales presentation. And music can be hilariously unsuitable. I remember attending a sales conference where the haunting strains of *Oxygène*, played as a nerve-tingling prelude, were totally incongruous with the company's new product: a disposable nappy. However, you could play a *short* dramatic piece of video: just enough to get attention.

Alternatively, a simple prop is very effective when handled with panache. Why not wear a pink carnation which, early in the proceedings, you dramatically pluck from your lapel and toss down, as you talk about 'dismissing outmoded attitudes'? My favourite Opener at seminars is to throw a diamond into the audience. Once the audience has politely handed it back, everyone assuming it's a fake, I go on to prove to them it really was a very valuable diamond indeed – and they are throwing away profitable opportunities like that every moment.

Less dangerous attention-getters for more solemn occasions are:

- **Ask a question.** If this is overdone, it will sound forced. In a large group, you'll get hands shooting up and down like a Nuremberg rally. But used skilfully, it gets you into the heart of the action fast:

  'How many people came here by car? [count]. And you all spent an average of one hour driving, right? That's thirty hours of non-productive executive time wasted already this morning, at a total cost to your company of over £500, isn't that correct? Suppose instead I could return at least £500-worth of value to your company right now? Well, here's an idea which could do just that . . . and it will take just five minutes of your time to explore . . .'

- **Promise an irresistible benefit.** (Let's assume you're selling a computerised time and payroll system.)

'If I could show you in the next twenty minutes a simple way to reduce your absenteeism by 25 per cent – without costing you a penny more than you're already spending – I'm sure you'd agree that that would be a worthwhile investment of your time.'

- **Shock statistics.** (Assume you're selling cold-store racking.)

  'Your cold store measures 25,000 cubic feet. You have told us that your racking system can hold only 15,000 cubic feet of product. That means, every moment we sit here you are pumping money into cooling 10,000 cubic feet of empty space. That adds up to a cost to you in wasted fuel of over £15,000 each year on this site alone – that's as much as 5 per cent of your net profits going to waste . . .'

- **News link.** (Assume you're selling financial services.)

  'You will all have heard this week of the grave problems facing small suppliers in the wake of the car strike. If you were a supplier to the car industry, you would be worried. You would be wondering. Shouldn't you be wondering right now . . . how *you* could meet your payroll if tomorrow your largest customer suddenly went out of business . . .'

- **Problem-solution.** (Assume you're selling truck washing systems.)

  'You have told us you want to reduce the cost of

washing your vehicles, cut the time taken, and make it easier for your staff to operate the washing system. We believe we have the answer to those three questions . . .'

- **Puzzle or suspense.** (Assume you're selling an advertising campaign.)

  'A key part of our brief was to develop a new corporate image for your company. Ladies and gentlemen, if that is your sole intention, I would advise you to leave now. Keep your money in the bank. We cannot help you.'

- **Human drama.** (Assume you're selling safety training.)

  'One of the grimmest tasks I ever had to perform was to attend a Coroner's Court, which was looking into the death of a construction worker. He was working 100 feet above ground, when the scaffolding collapsed beneath him. The scaffolding had, the Court found, been assembled incorrectly. Better safety training might have saved that man's life.'

- **Joke.**

  Dangerous! A joke usually has a victim in it somewhere and a failed joke (such as one with a mischosen victim) will hurt a sales pitch. Note too that some people have a perverse nose for the slightest whiff of imagined sexism or racism or anything-ism. Quotations are also risky. They are rightly perceived as chestnuts – unless you are giving an after-dinner speech, in which case half the audience will be in no state to perceive anything.

But it helps to cultivate all-purpose anecdotes. This one might go down well at Ever Ready (and then again, it might not. You can never tell with humour . . .):

> One day, the Marketing Departments of Ever Ready, Duracell and Vidor decided to make a pact with the Devil. They resolved to live on earth in luxury, enjoying the wonderful perks of their job, as long as their batteries kept selling. They all had confidence in their product, so they readily agreed. They all thought they'd live for ever.
>
> But soon afterwards, a question occurred to them. Nervously, Vidor asked the Devil, when uh, actually will Vidor batteries stop selling? The Devil grinned. By the year 1995, he said. Vidor wept. Duracell then asked, when will Duracell stop selling? The Devil laughed. By the year 2000, he said. Duracell wept. So Ever Ready asked, when will Ever Ready stop selling? The Devil looked into the future. And there was a very long silence. And then the Devil wept . . .

Quickly, you go on to say (amid tumultuous applause): 'and to make sure that Ever Ready keeps selling is what we're all here for today!' That story can be changed at will. For Ever Ready and the rest, insert the name of your audience's company – and their biggest competitors.

But be careful with humour. I believe that the textbook advice to 'open with a joke' really doesn't belong in a sales presentation. Whatever Opener you use, it's vital to link your Opener to the Body quickly with a statement such as: 'That means . . .', 'As a result . . .', 'For example . . .'

EFFECTIVE OPENERS

1. Ask questions

2. Promise benefit

3. Shock statistics

4. News link

5. Problem solution

6. Puzzle or suspense

7. Human drama

8. Joke or anecdote

How to preview your presentation

In your Opener, you should also establish a structure for the audience. And keep to it! It reassures them. If you deviate from your structure, the audience becomes uneasy, frustrated. If you cannot even keep your word on that, (they'll wonder) can your sales proposition be sound? Of course, you may have to deviate – for example in handling a question – but return from the deviation to your script *and show how it reinforces one of your key ideas.* Tie it back to the structure. For example:

> 'That question is particularly relevant, Mr Jones, because it brings us back again to the main benefit of our system, and that of course is . . .'

Your preview should ideally contain no more than three key points: the mind can't comfortably hold more than that at one time. For example: *your problem, our solution, the benefits* you will gain as a result. Or in the case of an information-only briefing for your own staff, the preview might cover the *present situation*, what we *plan* to do, and the expected *results*.

How to add credibility

Why should they listen to you? Perhaps your job function qualifies you. Or you have special experience. But it *is* important to give an answer to the unspoken question, why *you*? And then, why *your* company? Encapsulate your qualifications in just a sentence at this stage – you'll be expanding on them in the presentation.

> 'As you know, I was privileged to be the supervisor of the investigation which established why your company is experiencing these problems. I'll reveal our findings in just a few moments . . .'

Summary

- Define what you want to change in the audience – and establish what you can reasonably achieve in the time.

- Remember to establish the different objectives you have for different sub-groups.

- Your audience has a short attention span – structure your script accordingly.

- Write the Opener only after you've written the Close.

- Gain attention at once – but preferably not with a gimmick or joke.

- Add credibility to your Opener by explaining 'why *you*?'

5

Scripting the Body of your presentation – and the Close

'I am no orator, as Brutus is;
But, as you know me all, a plain blunt man.'
Julius Caesar, III, ii

Mark Antony's speech in *Julius Caesar* is typically held up as a model of persuasive rhetoric. And yet he did not use hyperbole or lavish metaphor or any of the gaudier tricks of rhetoric. The language is, in fact, very sparse. Only his structure is complex. He persuaded his audience because *he presented his facts and 'proof statements' in such a way that they could arrive at only one conclusion*. The most persuasive presentation is the one where the audience – like Mark Antony's – believes it has persuaded itself.

This is your principal task in the Body of your address. If you have written the Close first, then the Opener, filling in the middle (or the Body) is a lot easier. You know exactly where you're going, and coming from . . .

The classic presentation sequence (CPS) for the Body

Here is just one structure which has proven its credentials in persuading audiences:

- *Your Present Situation* – and why it's unsatisfactory. Why, in fact, it poses a real problem unless handled at once.

- *The Implications of your Problem* – and why they spell hidden and future problems for you too.

- *Our Solution* – and why it meets your immediate needs with tangible benefits.

- *The Implications of our Solution* – and why it offers hidden and future benefits too.

- *The Urgency of obtaining our Solution* – what you can lose by delaying. But what extra benefits you secure by acting now.

- *The Benefits* you gain (in summary) balanced against your low investment.

- *The Call to Action* (i.e. close the sale or gain the group's approval to advance one step further).

If you were selling cold-store racking to a big meat wholesaler, you might jot notes for your presentation like this:

> 'At the moment, you are paying to cool 10,000 cubic feet of cold store which is just empty space. That is wasting you £10,000 each year.

'With electricity costs going up soon, that cost will increase. Moreover, your production is rising and you are renting additional cold store space. Yet you already own that space in your own warehouse, if it could be made available.

'Our racking system will make full use of your cold store space, increasing your storage capacity by 5,000 cubic feet.

'All your expected production for at least the next two years will now be under your own control in one place, where it can be handled by your own experienced staff. You will no longer need to pay premium rates for rented storage space.

'Every week that you delay installing our racking costs you £200. How much product must you sell, to make that £200 which you are throwing away every week?

'We will have the racking installed within five working days, which means that you can enjoy immediately the convenience of having all your product under one roof. When you take into account the major savings you will gain, you will recoup your investment within six months and then every penny you save goes straight onto your profits.

'Give us the go-ahead now and we will start work this afternoon.'

P	THE CUSTOMER'S PROBLEMS
I	THE NEGATIVE IMPLICATIONS OF THESE PROBLEMS
C	THE CRITERIA ANY SOLUTION MUST SATISFY
T	HOW THE CUSTOMER SHOULD TEST ANY PROPOSAL
U	YOUR (U) PROPOSAL
R	BENEFITS WHICH WILL RESULT FROM YOUR PROPOSAL
E	EVIDENCE OF YOUR CAPABILITY

Another structure for the
Body of your
presentation

Remember this is a presentation for a major sale before a group of senior people. You've done your homework. If you were selling a minor item to an individual, you'd probably use quite different techniques. You'd seek Evidence of Customer Dissatisfaction ('Surely, all that wasted space is a terrible nuisance, isn't it?'), you'd attempt Trial Closes ('If it were available in red, would you buy it?' 'Would you rather receive 48 cases every month or twelve cases per week?'), you'd Probe for Mismatches ('Is it our easy payment terms or the initial order quantity you're not sure about?'). You'd do a lot of things.

If you use these techniques in a group presentation (except when handling a specific question), you're dead. Why? You're supposed to have researched the answers to all those questions before you called them together!

Instead, script your presentation according to the CPS pattern above. And throughout it, show in these ways how well you understand their problems:

Quantify the facts

Where possible, put figures against every point you make. 'You intend to increase your share of the bifurcated tin rivet market by 5 per cent in fiscal 1992 . . .' 'Your present vehicles will navigate aisles 1.5 metres wide, with a turning circle of 3.2 metres . . . However, you have told us that you require . . .'

You want your prospect to agree with you from the start: 'Yes, they've got the specification right.' Which underlines the importance of getting a very detailed spec beforehand, more facts than you need, if only to echo back their briefing in your presentation. This gives you another psychological advantage: 'Yes, they've listened closely to us, even the boring bits.'

Only try to get a consensus brief, one that *all* the decision-makers are willing to live with. Remember that each decision-maker has his or her own private agenda! I recall painfully the time one of our directors made a brilliant presentation to the board of a big travel company (whom she had not been able to meet before). At the end, they turned as one man to the Marketing Director (from whom she had taken the brief) and said: 'That was a good presentation, *but it wasn't what we wanted.*' Result: much time wasted on both sides.

Gain research in depth

One way to achieve this depth is to scrutinise their house journals, Annual Reports and corporate brochures. With notice, you can subscribe to an electronic information service to recover press clippings. ('As the *Financial Times* stated on March 3rd 1990, your early exposure in the Japanese market was well covered when you launched the XXXX range last year . . .')

Where relevant, you can make interesting calculations (from public-domain information) such as 'Your present net profit per employee is xxxxx . . .' 'Your current pro-ductivity per square foot of factory space is . . .' Chances are that your decision-makers do not know this them-selves! It gives you an incisive edge over your competitors.

Show how you meet their needs

If you were writing this as a sales proposal, your next section would be headed 'How product XYZ fulfils your needs'. You list the prospect's key needs again as para-graph headings – and you describe your product features, showing how they meet (perhaps more than meet) those specific needs. At the end of this section you have a heading: 'How you gain further benefits from the XYZ product'. Here you put the secondary sales points, such as longevity, maintenance, after-sales service, training, wide choice of styles or colours, etc. Detailing a wealth of intangible extras (all inclusive in the price) gives you a further plus over the competition, who may have the same extras but fail to detail them.

Anticipate the competition

What points will they make in *their* presentation? Remember I raised this vital point earlier! If they have advantages you cannot match, such as size, reputation, technical capability, sometimes you can undercut them – without mentioning the competition – by implying that such features have hidden weaknesses:

> 'The attention to fine detail you will find in the product finish, along with a low unit cost, is made possible because we make every part for you in our own local workshops. These are situated just fifteen miles from your company. Making all our own parts ensures the closest possible quality control, as well as fast delivery and a reliable after-sales service. We are committed to product quality, and that means we do not sub-contract.'

If you cannot scupper the competition in this way, better to ignore them and build on your own strengths. Or emphasise 'You get this and this, but also – you get ME.' That is, they get, not an anonymous 'big name' supplier who may lose their order or ignore their complaints, but a personalised service.

Make this concrete by saying 'Your primary consultant

on this contract is James Brown, whom we believe you know. James will always be available for technical advice during the commissioning period.' Dare you quote his home phone number? It helps!

Sell your 'hygiene factors'

Now that you've shown how your product more than meets their needs, and is better than any (unnamed) competitor's, tell them why your company is the one to buy from. In a written proposal you'd head this section: 'Why Smithy & Co is well qualified to serve you.'

Here you list the 'hygiene factors' in the sale. 'Hygiene factors' are what the prospect expects to find without asking, just as a company's employees expect to find clean washrooms, a safe work environment, and their wages paid promptly. The presence of hygiene factors alone will not normally close the deal – people do not buy from you because you have a Design Council Award, but because your product will do the job better. But a conspicuous absence of hygiene factors can kill.

So mention towards the end the key 'hygiene features' about your company and relate them to the customer's needs.

> 'Our clients include these names well-known to you.' [We'll gladly supply reference names and telephone numbers on request.]

> 'Our employees together have over 500 years of experience in [sheet metal fabrication].' [This means we can demonstrate the depth and breadth of skills

your supplier must be able to call on, to deliver the consistent quality you demand.]

'Our company was founded in 1968 and has steadily grown by 10 per cent each year to its current turnover of £5 million.' [We have the proven stability and excellent financial track record which you must have so that you can be sure a supplier will not go bankrupt on you. It is confirmed by the many companies which have for several years trusted us with major and long-term commitments.]

By stressing the right hygiene factors you can, of course, again undermine the competition. Complacently, they may have neglected to remind the prospect that they too 'have 500 years of experience', etc. Particularly if they haven't.

Dare you mention price at the start?

Budget, price and terms conventionally come at the end. Sometimes this can be a mistake. *If simultaneously reading your proposal, prospects will take one look at page one, then turn to the back page to see how much it all costs.* If it's more than they expected, they may not read or listen further.

You can pre-empt this, if you expect price resistance, by either not giving them the whole document till the end or by revealing the price at the front – just as a product *benefit*. 'At a low fixed cost, equivalent to just £40.76 per week, you gain these benefits . . .' Express it in small units. Show how the prospect need not pay it all at once. They will not be invoiced until the system is commissioned . . . or step-payments can ease the load. Perhaps they will gain all the product's benefits on Day One, and can put it to work building their profits at once.

Of course, these are sales points you will have explored in the initial meetings. *Emphasise them again.* Or the prospect will have forgotten (and his colleagues never have known) why the proposed capital investment of £10,000 is not so bad, if it yields a 10 per cent increase in revenue and a payback within just six months.

Here are yet more rules for scripting elegant Bodies:

Be just like them

Remember I said your audience trusts most those who are most like themselves? Or are most like what they want to be?

If you can't be a role model, at least establish that you have the same interests, needs and desires as the audience. 'We're all in this together.' For example: 'Our two companies have many things in common, above all the need to gain repeat business from our existing customers, and that calls for excellent service. Am I right?' The phrase 'Our companies have many things in common' implies 'I'm just like you!'

Don't challenge their existing beliefs

OK, I've already said that, but suppose, to make your

sale, you have to challenge them? I suggested that, if you must dislodge an old belief, go behind their belief and find the assumption that the belief rests on. Then show how your new idea actually reinforces the basic assumption. Here's how you do it . . .

For example: you are selling a new overnight distribution service. It costs more than their present seven-day delivery service and demands they hold higher stock levels. No longer will they have time to manufacture to meet orders. They must have stock available precisely when customers need it. Horror! they scream. High inventory means more working capital is tied up, which means lower profitability! Doesn't it? Not necessarily. It's a typical obsolete belief system.

Instead, can you show how the method reinforces their primary belief system – that maximum profitability is desirable? With faster deliveries, their retailers get the goods they want next day. So they can reduce *their* stock levels.

Suddenly, the firm with overnight delivery looks more attractive than other suppliers. So it can expand its market share, and increase off-take, which more than compensates for the working capital it has tied up in extra stock. And you also suggest ways it can better predict customer demand . . . and thus reduce its stock levels. Your way, it gains both ways . . .

Recognise the four 'audience types'*
and write accordingly

These traits are easily recognisable in individuals but they sometimes characterise entire groups. Advertising agencies research their audiences in this way to shape better ads, but I've yet to see many speakers consciously do it to shape a sales presentation. Whenever I've tried it, it seems to work!

These very broadly are the four audience types, and how to present to them:

Driver – Moves at fast pace, risk taker, loud, opinionated, rule breaker, assertive, poor listener. Entrepreneur. Dominant. At best, a leader of industry. At worst, a thug.

Your presentation should be strong, straightforward, highly structured, concise, full of bullet-point benefits, showing short-term results, the bottom line payoff, a choice of product options.

Expressive – Creative, imaginative, wild, an ideas-merchant, romantic, short attention span. Uses speculative 'imagine'-type language. At best, a visionary genius. At worst, an ineffectual dreamer.

Your presentation should be stimulating, 'imagine how . . .'; vigorous, motivational, full of unusual features,

*(I am indebted to Wilson Learning Corp. and The TRACOM Corp. for this model, initially developed for profiling advertising audiences.)

excitement, status, show opportunities for personal growth/recognition, emphasise fast results.

Amiable – People-oriented, lots of physical contact, name dropper, friendly gaze, shares personal feelings, uses 'feel' language. At best, a charmer. At worst, a creepy sycophant.

Your presentation should be friendly, relaxed, conversational, show features that help people/improve morale/ improve safety, show proof of your sound buyer–seller relationships, long service satisfaction, testimonials that stress service. Use people's names a lot.

Analytical – Detailed, orderly, pedantic, cautious, risk avoider, good listener, slow pace, limited small talk, time-disciplined, likes facts/specifics. Uses 'think' and 'read' language. At best, mind like a scalpel. At worst, a tax inspector.

Your presentation should be sober, logical, not threatening, painstaking, precise, punctilious on time and structure, pedagogic, stress integrity of your product, give tangible proof of all claims, guarantees, testimonials of industry gurus, documentation/lab results, proof of your personal competence and credentials.

These four traits are found to some degree in all of us. But they can also characterise entire groups or sub-groups. For example, sales people might be supposed to be amiable, accountants analytical, entrepreneurs drivers, creative people expressive, and so on.

When you single out these sub-groups to address individually, in the course of a presentation to the whole audience, take the trouble to script 'their' bit in the style they find most comfortable. They'll remember it. This can be your secret weapon when competing for the business against other presenters.

Type	How they appear	How to present
Driver	Fast-paced, impatient, assertive	Strong, terse, straightforward, clear options
Expressive	Creative, speculative, visionary	Imaginative, motivational, exciting
Amiable	People-oriented, feelings revealed	Conversational, personal, relaxed
Analytical	Cautious, slow paced, pedantic	Precise, painstaking, logical, conservative

Four ways to import credibility

Search for statistics, testimony of an expert witness, anecdotes, definitions of your terms. Let's imagine you're selling an advanced security system. Your credibility factors might include:

Statistics: 'Over 400 break-ins occur in offices in [Luton] every year. That's one for every ten offices. Statistically, it will be your turn at some time in the next ten years. But it *could* happen tonight . . .'

Expert: 'According to Scotland Yard, installing an alarm system of this kind can reduce the chance of false alarms virtually to zero.'

Anecdote: 'I recall one firm was losing 4 per cent of its stock through shrinkage or theft by its own staff. This fell to zero when it installed this security system. No longer could staff walk out the back door unobserved.'

Definition: 'Intelligent security is a system that can distinguish between real alarms and false alarms. It's like having a shepherd who can be relied on never to cry wolf unless it *is* a wolf.'

Be specific, graphic, concrete – not vague, theoretical or abstract. You probably don't remember Dr Goebbels' technique of the 'big lie' (I don't!). Nowadays we would call it 'disinformation'. But I understand that Berlin Radio would announce 'At Calais yesterday, 1224 British soldiers were killed and German soldiers are advancing victorious . . .' The first part was correct – the BBC would later confirm it. But the last part was usually a blatant lie. But the 'big lie' was accepted by many *because it was linked to an indisputable truth.*

I don't suggest you are in the business of disinformation. However, if you seek credibility attach precise figures, dates and sources to your statements. Why say 'the majority of companies choose our method' when with a little research you could prove it by saying '68 per cent of companies choose our method, according to a survey by *What To Buy For Business* in March this year (copies are included in your proposal)'?

Sustain interest

It helps to vary your type of material. One way – and you can do this quite methodically when editing your draft – is to switch in different types of attention-getter every few moments to reawaken people. A few moments after a paragraph of shock statistics, bring in a note of human drama. A few moments later, insert a puzzle or paradox. And so on.

But if you skip about to maintain interest, be sure to use a lot of connectives to tie your paragraphs together – 'As we've seen . . .' 'Now we'll examine . . .' 'Let's review. . . .' 'So much for that, now . . .' (Remember, the audience lacks the advantage of being able to read your material backwards and forwards to keep their place. You have to keep reminding them where they are in your structure.)

A simple way to sustain interest is to use short anglo-saxon words. (This test is not scientific, but it works for me . . . If you can add an 'eee' sound to the word and it sounds convincingly foreign, it probably is. Change it to blunt English.)

Another 'waffle killer' is to hit your point home with sharp jabs, often and tersely. Easily said, but . . . while we're all painfully aware of other people's waffle, how do you cut out your own waffle? Particularly as wafflers are usually sublimely unaware of their problem?

One idea is to rehearse with a tape recorder. And imagine you're talking to a customer in a pub. You wouldn't say 'to facilitate the progress of your order is usually a matter of little more than seven days'! You'd say sharpish, 'We'll turn your order round in a week!' Short sharp jabs and lots of them. Make the same few points but in different ways, using different examples. They concentrate the audience's mind.

Incidentally, don't be afraid to use the occasional cliché. They only became clichés because they deliver their message fast and memorably. There's no harm in saying 'After all, the name of the game is profit!' If it is.

The Close

People remember best what they heard first and last. It's

another reason why you should write the Close first. It's a template for the whole presentation *and* a call to action. So it should be very carefully scripted. Your Close should do this:

- Regain attention
- Return to opening theme
- Tell them you're about to close
- Summarise the ideas – five at most, ideally no more than three
- Re-establish your company's credibility
- Point to future benefits
- Call for action
- Finish up-beat, thank them and go

Then another member of your team can call for questions.

Summary

- The most persuasive presentation is one where the audience believe they have persuaded themselves – you can achieve this with careful structure.

- Script the Body of your address around a proven structure.

- Show them how well you understand their problems:
  Do research beforehand in depth.
  Demonstrate how you meet their needs.
  Anticipate the competition.
  Sell your 'hygiene factors'.
  Pre-empt price objections by mentioning price at the start.

- If you must challenge their existing beliefs show how your solution actually reinforces a primary belief on which their beliefs rest.

- Recognise that audiences come in four types – and write your script in the style appropriate to each.

- Use many 'proof statements' to strengthen your credibility.

- Sustain interest by switching in 'attention-getters' and by previewing and reviewing your script continually while you present. Audiences need to know at all times where they are in your structure.

6

How to 'stage manage' a presentation

'All my shows are great. Some of them are bad, but they're all great.'
Lord Grade

Have you ever been to a conference where a nervous speaker cowered behind the lectern? But the next one strode boldly among the audience, speaking fluently without notes? Then you'll know that there's a world of difference between a speech and a presentation. And the difference is stage management. It works at the smallest event as well as the mega-show. This part takes practice, but even if you're a first-time speaker you'll find that it's not hard to add a touch of panache. Here's how:

Maintain eye contact – gently

If you avoid their eyes it suggests, 'I don't believe what I'm saying'. But beware: if you confront them eyeball to eyeball, it's tantamount to a challenge. Accidental eye fixation can actually insult! A lady stalked out of my seminar room many years ago because – after I had made a general point that some customers are dishonest so we should beware of 'giving away the store' in sales promotions – my eyes rested accidentally on hers. Later, she told me she thought I was accusing her publicly of not paying her seminar fee! (She hadn't.)

A better idea is to look at their shoulders or ears. It's less challenging, but still appears personal. And switch your eye contact continually between the group members.

Also address individuals periodically by name. It keeps them awake because they never know whom you're going to descend on. Don't forget now and then to address with a smile your most enthusiastic group members. Their enthusiasm can be infectious! And sometimes it's nice to feel there's 'a friend at hand'.

Use voice control

Do you have a regional or foreign accent? Rejoice! Accents mesmerise an audience. They also add texture, allowing you to keep an audience awake longer. But even if your accent is BBC neutral, you can still simulate this texture:

- Speak more quickly than normal at the start. It unfreezes your panic, and commands attention. A funereal dirge sends out the wrong messages and you may never recover.

- Do *not* raise your voice to add emphasis. *Pause* . . . it implies that what's coming next is important. Or change the pitch of your voice – high becomes low and vice versa. Remember that dropping to a soft voice in places adds authority. It's a cheap trick, because people have to strain to listen to you. So make sure that what you say at these moments is specially important.

  Practise reciting a piece in a high, then low pitch, fast and enthusiastically or slow and solemnly. (Your secretary will think you're mad. Remind her that Churchill did the same, with his secretary present to take notes . . . Only he did it while in the bath!)

- Stop completely for five seconds just before you make your most important statement. Smile. Fiddle deliberately with a prop. This focuses the audience's attention completely on your next remarks. It's nearly as effective as striking a match, then holding it while it burns down to your fingers as if you've forgotten it. (This ploy is not recommended. Sometimes you do forget . . .)

Practise these ways to change texture and you'll be able to switch into them instinctively to add extra interest to your presentation whenever required.

Use body language – carefully

Gestures are wonderful, but they can be hilariously overdone, particularly by professional speakers. Then they look like hand jive. But used in moderation, they're valuable in adding animation to your address. If you're a Magnus Pyke, of course, you don't even need audio-visuals, you *are* an audio-visual. If you like gesturing – some speakers don't – make gestures like this:

- Slow, open gestures, palms towards audience, open arms, open hands? Yes! They say, 'Trust me.'

- Circular, sharing, open-armed movements? Yes! They say we're all in this together.

- Finger movements? Be careful. They can enumerate successive points 1, 2, 3 . . . (beware of how you indicate point two). But don't look like you're ticking off your audience.

- Avoid brisk, jabbing gestures; or closed fists; or chopping motions. They make your audience angry. Of course, you may want this, provided you can divert the anger outward at some unseen enemy. If you're an Arthur Scargill, your brisk jabs of the downward pointing finger will cue your applause before you've appeared to finish. It's a clever trick. It gives the impression that your audience is erupting with spontaneous enthusiasm. (This is an Advanced Technique. When Stalin used it, he took no chances. He stationed KGB guards in the audience to reinforce the enthusiasm.)

How to rehearse

Haven't we all seen the Chairman shamble towards the lectern, his notes on the back of an envelope? Of course, he hasn't rehearsed. Top people are far too busy. In fact, he probably didn't do badly with his envelope notes because he's made hundreds of speeches before and a sort of ponderous insensitivity develops its own style. But it wasn't a *presentation*, was it?

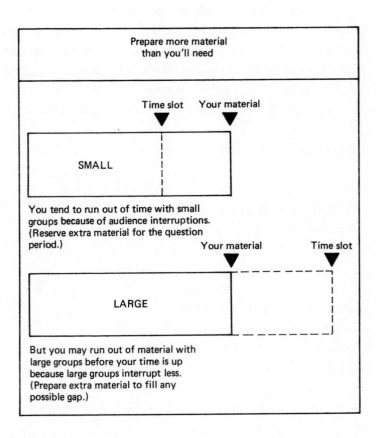

You must rehearse. If for no other reason than that it gives you the confidence that your material is *good*. Any glaring nonsenses have been cut out during rehearsal. Short of total systemic failure (like a fire evacuation) you know you will cope.

But don't rehearse once, rehearse three times – first, before a tape recorder (it forces you to perform, particularly if you set it to record and walk around it, gesturing). Second, rehearse before a friendly audience (for example, one's spouse, if friendly). Finally, rehearse before your critics (such as your business colleagues).

At the third rehearsal only, time your presentation. But don't trust your timing. Remember that a lot can happen on the day to throw your timing off. With a *small* group it may take a lot longer because of interruptions. So in this case, keep your presentation too short rather than too long.

But if you are presenting to a *large* group, there will not be many interruptions, if any. So if you speak quickly, under pressure of nerves, you could well run out of material half-way through your allotted time slot!

I remember one excellent seminar leader, whose materials had been more than enough for a full day in small, highly interactive groups, coming to grief at a large one-day event. His materials ran out before midday. The large audience had relaxed into Presentation rather than Workshop mode and did not interact. Together, we managed to fill the afternoon with hastily contrived exercises, syndicate presentations and group workshops . . . but it was a near thing.

Keep an extra five minutes (or five hours) up your

sleeve or on separate cue cards if there's any risk of your under-filling your time. *Do so anyway* . . . because it can give you fresh extra material to toss in during the question period.

Panic! Have you, despite all rehearsal, lost your place in your script? Wonderful! Don't panic or apologise. Welcome this refreshing break!

Pause. Take time to find your place and resume. The pause will look deliberate and professional and it will add texture. At worst, ask the audience to help you: 'What was that last point I was making?' 'Thank you . . . so what should logically come after that?' 'Thank you, and so it does . . .!' A contrived 'lost place' – well handled – can look like the height of professional scripting, even if it wasn't contrived.

Ask yourself now: What will I say, if I 'dry up' in front of the group? Just memorise a few fall back options and the panic abates. And remember, the audience *are* on your side.

But why take risks? Be belt and braces. Use cue cards. And if you're using overhead or 35mm slides, also write *their* contents on your cue cards. Then if your audio-visual equipment fails, you can at least salvage the presentation, by writing the visuals' contents on a flipchart or overhead acetate. It's messy, but better than total disaster.

So what about cue cards?

Write out your presentation as a script by all means.

Whenever I run an entirely new seminar, I write enough material for a book first. Then I reduce the book to notes, then the notes to cue cards. Likewise, when presenting a sales proposal, I write the notes in full, then distil them as single words on cue cards.

But do not take your notes or script to the presentation! You'll never be able to keep your place in them, and the pages will crackle in the microphone and look messy. Besides, a script insults the audience. They'll wonder why you didn't mail them the text beforehand.

A better idea is to jot just the key phrases on file cards – big capital letters in a dark felt-tip pen. Punch a hole in these cards at bottom left (so they rotate towards your body, rather than the audience, as you turn them over). Tie them together with string or plastic wire threaded through the hole. And number the cards (despite your best efforts, they'll get loose at some stage).

Code your cue cards prominently where your visuals come in, for example with coloured blobs. (I use big green dots to indicate an overhead slide, red for 35mm slide, and blue to cue an audience question or other departure from the formal presentation.)

Does all that sound as if you can stage-manage every event to your satisfaction? So you can – provided you are not inconvenienced with an audience. But audiences are unpredictable. Even the best ones will disturb your planned presentation, asking questions out of turn or leaping onto unscheduled topics. Occasionally, you may even have *trouble*. Here's how to handle it:

Handling unscripted moments – questions and interruptions

Listen closely to questions

Pause – it compliments the questioner. And acknowledge every interruption. Thank them. After all, there's no such thing as a bad question. Then restate the question to ensure you understand the point. It also buys you time.

Try to answer the question, not only to the letter, but also *in such a way that your answer illustrates a benefit.* 'That question is obviously important because if I can answer it to your satisfaction, you would feel happy about going one stage further with us, am I right?'

Script a few interruptions yourself

Ask a friend in the audience to plant a question, which raises a key benefit. If controlled, interruptions enhance the texture, and get the audience interacting. Your guests become the star of your show! But after interruptions be sure to summarise what went before and return to your sequence.

Anticipate your audience's worst questions and have an answer

Try to avoid that killer phrase 'I'll find out and come back to you'. (If you must, come back at once! Your sale is hanging fire meanwhile.)

Build answers to your audience's probable objections into the script

And show how the objections actually give you the opportunity to reveal key benefits.

> 'I'm sure that Mr Jones in particular [nods to Production Manager] will be concerned about quality control on the sub-contracted assemblies. I'll be frank, some suppliers will skimp on checking the quality of sub-contracted work. That's why we've built in our own special checks. They're unique to our process and they work three ways . . .'

Hold back a non-essential but valuable item for question time

Throw it in at the end. It can tip the balance, leaving your audience with a new benefit to consider rather than an objection.

> 'Sorry, didn't I tell you? We'll *guarantee* your delivery within 48 hours.'

> 'Of course, you can specify any colour you want on this order quantity at no extra charge.'

Handling difficult audiences

Yes, we all have them. You may occasionally get the problem guest even in small sales presentations in the prospect's boardroom. Don't be fast to dismiss irritating people. Sometimes they can be the cheque-signers.

I have invariably found that the delegates who ask the most questions at my sales presentations, and sometimes even hog the floor, are the ones who return the most glowing reports. And who recommend our appointment. *Because they were involved enough to ask questions.*

You can't win them all. (Two legendary seminar speakers – John Fraser-Robinson and John Winkler – once told me that they too always have a small percentage of delegates in every group that they can't satisfy, whatever they do. I felt vastly reassured!) However, you *can* handle most problems by recognising that, if you've got this far, your audience has a vested interest in getting value out of your presentation. So sweat to give it to them. And it doesn't hurt to show the sweat.

Moreover, at least one person in the audience (and probably the majority) *is on your side*. Those reasonable, patient individuals are the ones you address. Mentally. While answering the cranks. (I define a crank for this purpose as someone who makes clearly unreasonable demands on the group's time, in the opinion of the group. And you can tell that fact quite clearly, from the *group's* body language!)

Here's how to handle problem guests:

The speechmaker

They are not asking a question, really. Just hitting back at life's unfairness. So interrupt politely. Ask tersely for their question – and answer it.

If that doesn't work, remember that cranks really just want recognition. So give it to them. For example, John Winkler tackles speechmakers at his Pricing and Negotiating seminars by saying, 'go on, go on, tell us more, more . . .' until they run out of steam and the audience is hissing at them. He then acknowledges them very strongly and moves on.

If that fails, ask your group – 'shall we spend a minute to explore that?' and ask for a show of hands. Most cranks will buckle down, if the audience is clearly against them. If the audience says yes, invite your problem guest on the stage to present their case for one minute – and mobilise peer-group pressure in your audience to agree 'is exactly one minute fair?' It gets them off when the one minute is up.

In fact, most cranks will shrink in terror at the invitation to address the group 'from the chair'. However, it has been known for cranks to add entirely unexpected interest – and distraction – to the crucial last moments of a presentation. Which is why platform speakers at, say, a sales conference have been known to introduce their own, well-scripted 'crank' at the close – whose questions they can confidently answer with a resounding call to action!

The persistent interrupter

Say, 'Let's be fair to the others. We have a lot of ground to cover. Let's do a deal. We'll talk at the coffee break.' They won't talk later, because they really crave audience recognition.

The hostile critic

This is not a crank. He has a real problem with you. Show you understand his objection, and how you intend to handle it – perhaps in a separate discussion outside of the room. To him, it's important. Remember, the audience is always right. Never argue publicly with any individual! The audience takes it as an affront to them all and you lose them.

The private party and persistent noisy whisperer

Stop. Wait till they look up. Apologise, and say 'Sorry, I couldn't hear what you were saying.' Ask if they had a question or objection. Normally, with all eyes on them, they'll have the courtesy to shut up.

Several questions at once

In a large group, ask for the one main question – and answer it. Or you'll be there all day. But in a small group, if each is a valid sales objection, restate each one. Write each down on a flipchart and cross them off as you tackle them. Then ask – have I answered your questions?

Summary

- The easiest way to reinforce your sincerity in a small group presentation is to maintain eye contact.

- Use voice control – particularly pauses – for texture.

- Body language can add choreography to your presentation.

- You must rehearse three times.

- Cue cards – not scripts – are vital.

- Listen closely to questions and welcome them.

- Script a few interruptions yourself.

- Anticipate your worst questions and have an answer.

- Build answers to your audience's probable objections into your script.

- Prepare yourself in advance to handle 'difficult' audiences.

7

How to cope with disasters

A speaker was hired to address a press conference, but when he turned up only one journalist had arrived. Still, the organisers insisted he begin. After ten minutes, he stopped and turned to the one journalist and said, 'This is a bit silly. Are you sure you want me to carry on?' 'Absolutely, old boy,' the 'journalist' said.'I need to know all this. I'm the next speaker.'

Don't worry, you'll never have a disaster. The easiest way to guarantee that is to prepare for disaster at every presentation you make. Disasters come in different guises, of course. When hosting a public event, like a press reception, the panic over whether your equipment will work may be reduced to total insignificance by the question: will anybody even turn up? (Solution: invite three times more than you need, and phone them all the day beforehand.) At least at a sales presentation you can usually count on having an audience. *Now* your worries may well include, will the equipment work?

One of the best reasons for making your presentation in your own offices is that you can be sure it will. You control the environment. No need to fret about the audio-visual gear breaking down (you have a replacement) or the screen collapsing (you checked it last night) or the coffee failing to arrive (your own secretary is hovering with it at the door) . . .

This confidence itself can give you an extra tangible 'edge' in closing the sale. Conversely, an uncontrollable environment can destroy even the best-planned presentation.

For one of my earliest big sales presentations, we chose a certain well-known hotel beside Heathrow airport – conveniently close to the client's premises. In the course of two hours, the fire alarm went off twice, the adjacent kitchen clattered dishes non-stop, the projector bulb blew (and it took thirty minutes for the hotel to replace it), jumbo jets took off overhead every three minutes destroying all dialogue, the air conditioner alternatively roasted and froze people, and that was the least of it.

The air carried unmentionable odours from the nearby sewage farm, and guests' cars were blocked in by tourist coaches on departure! Yet the place had looked so good, and its terms so reasonable, on my inspection tour . . . (No, we didn't get the business.)

Some ten years, 240-plus presentations and thirty or so big-name hotels later, I have found *only two hotels* in Britain which really understand the needs of business meetings (names on application!). I can trust them to do at least these three things, which hotels should carry out routinely for business presentations (but don't):

- Have a senior manager continually in attendance during the vital set-up stage. (Forget trying to find a porter to urgently replace a light bulb or furnish an extension lead. They're always 'somewhere in the building' ferrying luggage.)

- Supply, set up and *test* equipment before handing it over, so we don't have to wrestle with it. Or sweat at 9 am for its replacement to arrive, just as the guests are sitting down.

- Tape down electric leads, so guests don't trip. (When was the last time a hotel did that for your meeting, unprompted?)

Of course, there's more to venue management than that. But for me, those three points separate the professional meetings hotels from the amateurs. Some of Britain's most prestigious hotels I would not trust to set up a lemonade stand.

One answer to snafus outside your control is to anticipate them. Remember, if you're presenting at the customer's premises, poor presentation facilities are virtually inevitable.

Pack spare extension leads . . . plug fuses and adaptors . . . projector lamps . . . batteries . . . Sellotape . . . Blu-Tack . . . a soft pad to protect the customer's boardroom table from your 35mm projector . . . two little wooden blocks or ashtrays to prop up said projector (never has a projector been focused properly without the help of two ashtrays, but this fact apparently remains unknown to all projector manufacturers!) . . . whiteboard pens . . . acetate pens . . . scissors . . . plyers . . . stain remover and coat brush (sod's law says, you will discover soup stains on your suit just before you're called before the spotlights).

If you make a habit of business presentations, you could keep a permanent Emergency Kit like this in your car.

If despite your preparation, the worst happens, here are some tips for handling it:

Don't panic and don't apologise

At least, not at once. If your equipment totally fails and you can't go on, explain to the audience why. Most will sympathise. Confidently declare a ten-minute break. Get the hotel (or your host, if presenting at a client's venue) to fix the errant item. Your audience will probably be glad of the break. (But assign a colleague to recall them from the temporary sanctuary they've found in the bar or their in-trays.) The key is: be confident. Audiences will forgive you almost anything except not being told what's happening and why.

If it's a minor débâcle, like a projector breaking down, say – as the TV news presenters do – 'we'll come back to that later'. Dispatch a colleague for help and move briskly on. Behave as if it's part of the show, as if you welcome the interruption.

It helps to prepare standard joke responses to likely emergencies. They get audience sympathy (the weakest joke on these occasions will win laughter), and you can also enlist the audience's active help. For example:

Off noises – 'Are they banging to get in or banging to get out?' 'This is an extra-value presentation, folks: you get poltergeists as well.' Then deputise a guest to shut them up!

Faulty equipment – 'Everything's working fine, folks. We just didn't pay our union dues.' Or 'Obviously, my guarantee just ran out.' Now ask, 'Is there an expert in the house?' There always is . . .

And the **all-purpose disclaimer:** 'Does this ever happen at your presentations? Isn't it a pain? Any suggestions as to what I should do?' *Invite the audience to help you* – change bulb, erect fallen screen, collect tumbled props, uplift fainted delegates, whatever . . .

Small disasters can actually help you. They break the ice. When the air conditioning failed at a Manchester present-ation, we opened the windows. The wind blew guests' papers all over the room and during the scramble to col-lect them from beneath chairs and tables, our people and theirs got to know each other with amazing speed.

Major disasters are something else – at least, unless you can invoke the powers of genius to recover quickly. For example, I remember well the day the Chief Executive of a giant corporation marched onto a conference platform before 800 senior executives, raised his arms, said 'Wel-come' – and fell off the stage. He picked himself up, returned to the rostrum with a wry smile, and said: 'That just shows how we can all fall down, if we don't keep our feet firmly on the ground. And that's what this day is all about!' He was the star of the show. Uproarious applause! A place in the company's Hall of Fame!

Alas, it didn't happen that way at all. Mortified with

shame, he *stayed on the ground* throughout the opening cere-
mony, and the sad occasion passed into the company's
folklore.

Shrug disasters off, learn what you did wrong, and use it
to improve your next performance. It's not the end of the
world. There are other jobs, other countries . . . Besides, I
jest. Usually nobody but you and your nearest colleagues
will care that much. Sometimes, that's the hardest part to
accept. And anyway, perhaps the 'failure' is just in your
own mind.

I remember a client who appeared on a regional TV
news programme – live. Purely out of nerves he made a
(what seemed to him) slanderous comment about his
Managing Director. That night, he slunk home. He wrote
his resignation letter. He appeared at the office late next
morning to return his car – only to find the company feting
him as a hero! Nobody had noticed his 'disaster'.

Remember Churchill. He failed at everything. He failed
at school. He failed in the army (he got captured by the
Boers). He sent thousands of soldiers to their death in the
Dardanelles, a military fiasco. He precipitated a mone-
tary crisis by returning England unwisely to the gold
standard. So great were his failures that they made him
Prime Minister. Doesn't your so-called 'failed' presentation look just a bit trivial by comparison?

Summary

- Assume the worst will happen, and prepare for it.

- Don't panic – welcome the novel snafu or interruption as if it's part of the show!

- Don't apologise (at least, not at once).

- Invite the audience to help you.

- Don't worry too much about a 'disaster' – its worst aspects by far may be merely in your own mind.

8

How to use audio-visuals

'They display most, who have the least to say'
Matthew Prior

The value of audio-visuals is that, according to research, their use doubles the amount of information which sinks into your guests' minds and the length of time they can recall it afterwards. Perhaps this is because audio-visuals appeal to both sides of the brain. The left brain processes your logic, while the right brain admires your pictures and sounds. When both brains compare notes, the material sinks in faster and stays longer.

Of course, that's just a buzz-speak way of saying that audio-visuals add variety and interest and help keep audiences awake. Which we all know anyway . . .

Even so, it is difficult to sustain peak attention longer than seventeen minutes and sometimes audio-visuals can actually hurt your presentation. The after-lunch slot is the worst time to turn off the lights and put on a slide show – you'll hear snores. And if you want to destroy your presentation, start with a thirty-minute video – one that's all about *you*. Why should they care? You'll hear worse than snores.

Timing can be more important than visuals, in holding attention. Sharp at 9 am is often the best time to stage your presentation. They're fresh and they haven't had time yet to get distracted by the day's crises. It also looks crisply efficient. Attention slumps in late morning and if your meeting starts around 11.30 am, who takes who to lunch? Settling this matter at the outset will concentrate their minds . . . Attention rises after 3 pm but beware a slot as late as 4.30 pm when your presentation will be truncated by those who must leave early.

Types of audio-visual

If yours is the sort of company which cannot present without a twenty-foot video wall or a show involving ten synchronised projectors, you'll need another sort of book than this. You'll also need a team of technicians and a budget like a pop star's ransom.

But most seasoned presenters still prefer portable, simple equipment that they actually understand – and which they can cope with personally if it fails. Here are the kinds you're most likely to meet, with guidelines on which works best and where.

Carousel 35mm projector

Once, this was my favourite stand-by for groups from six to sixty. It's very flexible. With a remote control device in your hand, you control the presentation at your own pace. You can maintain a back-up library of slides for all occasions and customise a slide show to a particular customer in a few minutes.

A tip: avoid storing vast quantities of mounted slides. Mounts are costly, slippery and bulky. Instead, keep slides unmounted in stamp albums – the archival kind which have little pockets. You can store thousands in a few cubic inches, complete with index, and mounting slides on demand takes only seconds.

If you're presenting at the client's premises, most clients can muster an ancient projector plus screen or, at worst, a blank wall (although you'd be well advised to bring your own complete gear).

But nowadays I'm less sure about the value of slide projectors . . . you can't see projected slides well in a large room unless you import a fabulously noisy extra-power projector. Many rooms cannot be blacked out and adjusting the lighting is often a hopeless task, even in so-called hotel 'conference suites'.

The machine whirs and distracts your audience, unless you use a back projection screen which demands more depth than most rooms offer. Bulbs usually blow at the worst moment (so check you're using a projector with an integral spare lamp you can flick across in a moment). Slide trays easily jam, particularly if you're using cardboard or cheap plastic mounts.

Worse, they have a habit of losing their lids and scattering their contents, just moments before your presentation. To guard against this, number every one, even if you only have three in a tray!

Moreover, slides are very expensive if you do them professionally and it can be a false economy to produce them yourself, at least if your budget and needs are small. But what about homemade Polaroid slides? At this date, the monochrome varieties offer acceptable quality for professional presentation, but the colour slides simply do not.

A graphics program on your personal computer sounds fine in principle: you just photograph images off the screen. However, you'll need a fine resolution monitor (2400 lines minimum), which may cost more than your computer. You need to produce a lot of slides to justify it. The poor line resolution on your TV or standard computer monitor just won't do!

Of course, you can photograph your own artwork using a tripod and two strong copier lights. Given time and temper, this option is very inexpensive. You can make coloured text slides which are acceptable for some purposes, simply by using typed headlines which you photograph using colour slide film, a macro lens and a colour filter on your camera. But too often, homemade slides look it . . .

A low-cost compromise is to pay a slide bureau, one using computer graphics, to prepare you a library of standard text and graphic slides. These are ones that keep reappearing in your presentations. Then you buy just a few 'customised' slides, specific to any given presentation, when you actually need them.

But make sure you order at least one duplicate set of your standard slides. It will cost you little if ordered at the same time. Otherwise, what will you do when the Chairman leaves your master set on the train?

Portable desktop projectors

These are the ones like televisions with their own screen. They're fine for boardroom-style presentations but can be watched comfortably by no more than ten guests at most. Better value are the kind which, at a touch, can also project onto an external screen, allowing presentations to be seen by up to twenty people. Some also have internal audio recording, playback and editing facilities, so you can pulse your soundtrack to trigger the slides automatically and thus produce your own little *Son et Lumière*.

If I had to use 35mm slides, I'd invest in one of these. But, unless it was important that the tape-show feature somebody who was *not* present at the meeting, I'd turn the soundtrack off – and talk the slides through personally. Why play monkey to your own organ grinder?

Overhead projectors

Another familiar standby, they are as flexible in use as a 35mm slide projector but have (I believe) more advantages. First, the slides are cheaper to make (a bureau can produce a full colour A4-sized transparency at around £6 each from your flat artwork or even from your 35mm slide).

Of course, you can instantly prepare your own monochrome text and graphics slides on the office photocopier for just a few pence, and slides in colour too if you have access to a colour photocopier.

They let you dispense entirely with a flipchart or whiteboard when writing key points. You simply write on clear acetate slides on the projector itself. (Use washable pens and you can even wash and recycle the slides. Over a period this will save you significant sums against the cost of replenishing flipcharts.)

Overhead projectors are far more reliable than 35mm projectors. They can't jam, are quieter in use and you can see what they project even in a well-lit room. So they're ideal for large presentations, even to many hundreds of guests. (For the largest rooms, hire a high-power projector of 4000 lumens.)

But beware the portable 'pack away' projectors. Their light output is small and your darker slides will just not get projected. Also you need to clothe their reflective screens in velvet, they scratch at a glance.

Of course, one drawback of unmounted overhead transparencies is that they slide around like a family of eels, so you'd best frame (and number) them. This makes them more bulky than 35mm slides. However, if you put your presentation notes on the cardboard frames, you can run an entire presentation off them and it looks very impressive – as if you're talking without notes!

Alternatively, you can seal the transparencies permanently in clear plastic sleeves, the kind with punched holes at the side. Store these in a ring binder. Then you can assemble a binder-full of slides in sequence for each presentation and put each slide, sleeve and all, on the projector when required. Moreover, the plastic sleeve stops the slide inside from buckling under the projector's heat.

Video films

I believe more presentations have been lost by video than

won. We gained a big account when presenting against one of the largest PR companies in Britain, because (the client told us later) they started with a prestige twenty-minute video of *their* company and the client went to sleep. Instead, we started by talking about the *client* – and we picked up the business.

The benefits of showing a video film are that it under-lines your stability and professionalism ('so you can afford video?'). It can give superb demonstrations of complex processes, figures or facts, probably more convincingly than you'll manage with felt-tip and flipchart. And it's indisputably an attention-getter, at least for a few minutes. Customers like to watch a 'show'.

The drawbacks are that video is no longer novel (we all watch TV and some of us have home video cameras). Video films made for commercial presentations are inva-riably too long (even five minutes is a long time to watch a TV screen, given the usual clichés of corporate flag-waving to which these films are prone). Above all, it is difficult to customise a video film to a specific customer at reasonable cost, and the all-purpose corporate video soon becomes outdated. Besides which, producing one major video film can equal one office move, in terms of expense and executive anxiety!

One of our own clients has had success in laying a *custo-mised* soundtrack over a professionally produced video which shows the *standard* features of his service. Of course, the customer's name features repetitively in the soundtrack. It looks as if the entire film was shot just for that one presentation. Remember the commercial for the local garage or Chinese restaurant last time you went to the cinema? Of course, it was a customised soundtrack dubbed onto standard film footage. Is this a clever idea for your next business video too?

I believe the worst kind of video film (unless you're selling videos) is one where every gimmick of computer graphics is displayed. And instead of buying your product, the customer says, 'Wow – we need a video like that. Who made it for you?'

Audio

Don't overlook opportunities to incorporate sound recordings, such as brief interviews made with his prior consent with the customer's dealers or potential users or his own customers (or even his staff). A soundtrack switched on at intervals from a simple cassette player adds novelty and texture. You can even make a high-fidelity recording of telephone interviews, by taking a lead from the mouthpiece microphone in the telephone headset directly to the microphone input of your recorder.

Flipcharts

These are amazingly costly to produce, using a professional signwriter (who invariably can't spell). They also tend to cascade around your feet in sheaves of paper. Really, they are more apt to an internal presentation, where you can add notes as you go. If you must use them, learn to ticket-write professionally yourself – learning it takes all of fifteen minutes from a signwriting book.

Display cards

These are good for intimate round-table presentations. You type headlines and terse notes on the office word processor, enlarge them on a photocopier and stick them on to stiff cards about twelve inches square. Display them on a desk-top easel. One set I made in an hour or two, very cheaply, helped us bring in a £100,000 contract. They are best displayed in conjunction with a written proposal so the customer can refer to the details as you go.

Microphones

You won't need them in small groups and they can be a nuisance in large. Fixed mikes are a curse to the confident speaker: they tether him or her to one ineffectual spot, which is usually behind the lectern.

Novices tend to make love to the mike, nervously holding it to their lips the way they see pop singers do. This distorts the sound. Besides, spit destroys the mike (you probably haven't got a pop singer's budget!). It will pick up your voice far better if you stand back and speak normally. A mike is adjusted properly if you can't hear your own voice coming from the speakers. If you can, you're holding it too close or it's set too high.

A roving mike on a lead gives you the option to wander about, but if you do, be sure to prepare a standby joke about 'falling down on the job'. Because you will. The lead will appear to go out of its way to trip you.

A hand-held radio mike is far better, but keep a watch on the batteries. They run out after just an hour or two. A battery-powered tie mike is better still. Look ma – no hands. However, few venues are equipped to handle it without hiring in a raft of special equipment; and remember it's live – your *sotto voce* remarks will be broadcast!

Seven quick tips for using audio-visual successfully

Bring your own equipment

The customer's promised gear is always absent or knackered. And don't forget your Emergency Kit (see earlier).

Arrive early and insist on adequate time to set up, so your half-erected display screen doesn't collapse onto the antiques under the Chairman's fretful eye. If you must set up while the customer's team watches, find a way to involve them. Perhaps they can focus the projector while you hold the screen. Or they can plug in the remote lead. Or they can comment on visibility from the back . . .

Put the customer's name on the visuals

Do it on the first visual and thereafter. Where you would normally put a blank slide or flipchart page, between sections of your presentation, put a picture of the customer's logo. People like looking at their own name. And it says, this is *your* presentation. (For the same reason, put their name at the top of every page of your documentation too.)

Make your visuals dynamic

This doesn't demand complex gimmickry. Just let the visuals develop as they watch. The acetate slides used on overhead projectors do this very well. You can overlay as many as six slides, to build successive stages of a bar chart or to project sales figures year by year or to illustrate the planned growth of a customer project.

Another idea is to pre-write parts of graphs or tables on acetates, then write in the remaining details as they watch. Or you can fit out an acetate with little window flaps. You uncover successive parts of the acetate as you go, until the whole picture is revealed.

Of course, you can achieve the same effects rather more arduously with 35mm slides or even flipchart pages. (If you intend to write on your flipcharts, trace the words or graphics beforehand in fine pencil. It makes you look as talented as Rolf Harris . . .)

Lay out the room for easy display

Set out your display equipment so you can take your slides from the left and put them on the overhead projector at your right (if you're right-handed). Arrange a top table to one side of the screen to hold your notes and materials, and to rest your remote lead. Obvious? No . . .

If you leave the room layout to someone else, chances are you'll have no choice but to march back and forth a dozen yards between a top table and the projector, scattering your materials as you go and obscuring the screen! It also pays to use a retractable pointer, rather than those little lights which dance around the screen or – worse – a pencil which may mark or tear it.

Keep text visuals simple

A few key words or phrases per slide are all your audience can comfortably digest, while still paying attention to what you're saying. Incidentally, use enlarged *lower case* for slide text. It's far easier to read than upper case.

Don't make the visuals dominate

Or you'll end up out of pocket, and with a customer who says 'What a show! But what did it say?' You'll also lose spontaneity – the chance to stop for questions or handle objections while they're burning a hole in the audience's attention.

Don't take the equipment down until your presentation is over

It signals 'end of session'. For the same reason, avoid turning your projector off and on during the presentation. (Besides, this may blow the fuse or the bulb.) It's safer to put on a blank slide – bearing the customer's name and logo – during long pauses, if you're worried about your audience being distracted by a white screen.

Summary

- Assume the customer's promised equipment won't materialise – bring your own.

- Emphasise the customer's name – not yours – as the most dominant element of the visuals.

- Make your visuals dynamic, developing a story as you present.

- Lay out the room the way *you* want it.

- Keep text visuals simple.

- Don't make the visuals dominate.

- Don't take the equipment down until your presentation is over.

9

Writing the sales document

'Making a sales presentation without literature is like
hunting a tiger with your bare hands. Yes, it can be done,
by why do it?'

Anon.

'I close all my sales personally,' you say. 'My leave-
behind literature is just a formality.' Um . . . Yet your
proposal or tender document *is a sales presentation* – on
paper! It will probably be read by people you've never
met, who didn't attend your presentation. Did someone
say that every major sale requires at least five presentations – and the consent ultimately of at least five key
decision-makers? Of whom, you will only have met but
two or three? *So your proposal must be able to stand on its own.*

Of course, the format may be rigidly defined for technical specifications, or for tender documents for certain
kinds of work (or customer, such as the government).
However, even within the limits of accepted practice, a
proposal document can (and should) sell its heart out.
Here are eight ways . . .

Personalise . . . personalise . . .

Write the name of the company *and the individuals* to which you are presenting, on page one. As we've seen, people are mesmerised by their own name. And weave in the name of their company throughout the document, in such a way that this does not merely appear to be a trick of word processing. Acknowledge by name in the Preface all those among the prospect's staff who assisted you in your briefing.

Remind them of their needs

Your first section is headed: 'Your Objectives (or Requirements)'. Start by restating their company's objectives or needs in great detail. As a trained sales person, you are acutely aware of the need to find the customer's key needs. And to *match* them with your product benefits. And to probe for the areas of mis-match, until the prospect can agree 'Yes those are all my needs – and if you can supply them, I see no reason why we shouldn't proceed.'

So your proposal should restate these grounds for agreement. You have already determined these grounds, in your pre-presentation research. *Logically, if you can show a full match, they must say yes.*

Follow the Classic Presentation Sequence (CPS)

We saw how the CPS should structure your verbal presentation. The CPS – plus all the other points mentioned in that chapter – makes a fine pattern for your sales document too.

Your Appendix sells too

Don't forget one! It's like the PS in a direct mail letter, sometimes the second thing people read – after the introduction. It helps to have this photocopied on different coloured paper. Here are all the extra 'credibility' factors you can muster. Guarantees. Reprints of suitable press articles extolling you. Customer testimonials. A client list. Technical specifications.

Make it look important

Bind it in a professional way, even if this costs you. Every buyer can recall documents, submitted for work worth a five-figure sum or more, held together by rubber bands or paper clips. A business-like and carefully selected binder will stand out when the prospect scans his stack of competing proposals. It will also summarise your company's style. So hand-tooled leather may be 'over the top'

– particularly if presenting to a local government body. A good quality artboard cover, with your name embossed, and the pages 'perfect bound' in a heatsealing machine or by your printer could be just right.

Remind them of the points they made

If you have made the presentation in person, write them another letter the very next day, in which you reinforce your main selling points again – particularly if you can refer positively to questions raised at the presentation. 'Taking the point which Mr Harvey raised, I confirm that we will guarantee delivery within 48 hours . . .' When a prospect is teetering between two proposals, this evidence of your attention to detail may win the day.

Thank them for the business

If yours is a business which relies on repeat or future sales (and whose doesn't?), remind the customer *after the sale* of the benefits of doing business with you. Send a letter to your decision-maker, thanking him for the business, and softly reciting again the benefits he will now gain. Make your invoice a selling document too. For example, list on the invoice all the delivery, testing, commissioning and similar services you would expect to give free anyway – and against them write, 'No charge'.

Gain a testimonial

Some months after the sale, contact the customer to gain a written testimonial. Not only is this invaluable for your future selling, but also the mere act of asking the customer to recite the benefits he has gained cements them in his mind. He can reassure himself he has made the right decision. He has also made a public commitment. He is less likely to switch to your competition.

Summary

- Personalise the sales document with *their* name throughout.
- Remind them of the brief they first gave you, in case the goalposts have moved since.
- Follow the Classic Presentation Sequence (CPS) for your sales document.
- Don't forget an Appendix for your 'hygiene factors'.
- Make it look important (it is).
- Remind them afterwards of the points *they* made at your presentation.
- Thank them for the business – if you get it.
- Gain a testimonial from your newly satisfied customer.

Appendix: Improving your performance

Feedback questionnaire: after the rehearsal

This list is helpful if circulated for your colleagues to use after your final rehearsal. It checks *how* you came across:

1. Overall, how did the speaker appear? Confident/not confident . . . in command of the material/not in command . . . convincing/unconvincing . . . how else?

2. Use of body language . . . stiff or relaxed, gestures, what did the body language say?

3. Use of notes . . . closely scripted or relaxed/ spontaneous?

4. Eye movement . . . roving or static, up or down, who did it target? What did it convey?

5. Voice level . . . varied in pitch and pace? Or monotonous?

6. What style of presentation predominated: amiable (people-orientated) or analytical (facts/logic), driver (direct, blunt) or expressive (discursive-imaginative?) How relevant was that style to the audience – and the sub-groups?

7. What emotion was conveyed: enthusiasm, inspiration, conviction? Or was it a recitation?

Feedback questionnaire: after the event itself

After the presentation itself, ask your colleagues to evaluate your *strategy* according to these questions. And ask them also of yourself:

1. Did I have the audience analysed right?

2. Was my presentation well targeted to the group and sub-groups?

3. Did the presentation achieve its purpose?

4. Was my evidence relevant and effective?

5. Was my delivery persuasive and did it hold attention?

6. Did the visual aids add to the presentation?

7. Did the questions at the end move us towards a sale?

In particular, ask your colleagues what aspects could be improved next time?

Feedback questionnaire

The checklist overleaf reviews the content of your presentation. Because each content is radically different, I leave it to you – following the experience of this book – to set the goalposts:

PERSUASIVE BUSINESS PRESENTATIONS

Content	Best aspect?	What could be improved? How?
Opening		
Body		
Close		

Most
effective
proof
statement:

General
comments
on improving:

Bibliography

Elsea, Janet, *The Four Minute Sell*, Arrow Books, 1984.

Fast, Julius, *Body Politics*, Tower Books, 1980.

Jay, Antony, *Effective Presentation*, Management Publications Ltd., 1970.

Jeffries, James R. and Bates, Jefferson D., *The Executive's Guide to Meetings, Conferences and Audio-visual Presentations*, McGraw-Hill Paperbacks, 1983.

Kennedy, Gavin, *Everything is Negotiable*, Arrow Books, 1982.

Korda, Michael, *Success!*, Ballantine Books, 1977.

Murray, Sheila L., *How to Organise and Manage a Seminar*, Prentice Hall Inc., 1983.

Robinson, Nick, *Marketing Toolkit*, Mercury Books, 1989.

Turner, Barry T., *Effective Technical Writing and Speaking*, Business Books Ltd., 1974.

Winkler, John, *Bargaining for Results*, Pan Books, 1987.

Zimmer, Marc, *Effective Presentations*, Sphere, 1987.

Presentation and Marketing Training, available from The Marketing Guild, 482 Dunstable Road, Luton LU4 8DL (Tel: 0582 490430).

The Mercury titles on the pages that follow may also be of interest. All Mercury books are available from booksellers or, in case of difficulty, from:

Mercury Books
W.H. Allen & Co. Plc
Sekforde House
175–9 St John Street
London EC1V 4LL

Further details and the complete catalogue of Mercury business books are also available from the above address.

Nick Robinson's

MARKETING TOOLKIT

Nick Robinson's *Marketing Toolkit* is an encyclopaedia of more than 1000 fresh, tested marketing ideas to improve your business success.

This intensely practical book illustrates a wealth of ingenious new ways for your organisation to create profitable sales. It details advertising approaches – including displays, classified, loose inserts, directory, product cards and local radio. It reveals direct marketing methods, including ways to boost direct mail and direct response advertisements. And it gives specific step-by-step guidance in planning, budgeting and executing effective sales lead generation programmes.

All organisations can profit from these ready-to-go plans, regardless of their type of market or size of budget. And any reader who has the task of making marketing succeed – whether you direct other people or do the job yourself – will benefit from this down-to-earth advice, based on the author's 20 years' personal experience of what actually works.

ISBN 1 85251 002 1 (hardback)

TURNING PRACTICAL COMMUNICATION INTO BUSINESS POWER

Bernard Katz

Good communication is a direct pathway to the ingredients of business power. Effective communicators exert influence. They establish authority, promote understanding, and they persuade. Good communications is as essential to the corporate body as it is to the individual manager.

In his latest book Bernard Katz provides the reader with a range of practical communication skills. They apply to the three major areas of business:

- The company communicating with its customers and public

- Management and staff communicating with each other

- The individual manager and executive who must make personal presentations, conduct meetings, prepare reports, promote a product of service, and communicate professionally on the phone.

Getting better at communicating is easy. There are examples, with check lists and rules, and dire warnings of what not to do. Guidance is also provided for the selection of audio-visual back-up to the communication message. And there is a section, with training guidelines and examples, for those whose task is to train others to communicate more effectively.

Turning Practical Communication Into Business Power is essential reading for all concerned with promoting and manipulating business understanding. It pays particular attention to the private apprehensions of those learning to overcome communication pitfalls.

ISBN 1 85251 076 5 (hardback)

WINNING WAYS

James Pilditch

How has Alan Sugar grown from selling car aerials off the back of a truck to owning one of the most successful companies in the world? How did Anita Roddick, a 33-year-old housewife with two children, become Business Woman of the Year? What does a firm in the Staffordshire countryside (JCB) do to be market leader in 56 countries? What gives Sony and Sharp and Canon and Minolta their edge with customers? Why are IBM and Philips and Courtaulds and Honda always in the lead?

Winning Ways is written for all who want their businesses to do better – directors, engineers, designers, marketing, R & D and financial people – and for educators who, as the book suggests, have a larger role to play.

'James Pilditch has produced a book which should be compulsory reading for managers. Britain has the conditions now which enable its manufacturing industry to survive. What we need is many more winning products. James Pilditch has shown the way to get them.'
Sir Simon Hornby, chairman W H Smith, chairman Design Council

'. . . very nicely instructive, full of strong examples and focused reasoning. I especially like the fast-paced urgency that moves the reader along as he constantly gets helpful new advice and insights. The book should be a winner.'
Theodore Levitt, Editor, *Harvard Business Review*

'In this wonderfully clear book it becomes obvious that the author is a man of vision . . .'
Robert Heller

ISBN 1 85252 042 6 (paperback)